AF480602

Getting Ready for My Plane Ride™

An Airplane Book for Kids

This book belongs to:

____

Written by Dr. Fei Zheng-Ward   Illustrated by Moch. Fajar Shobaru

Copyright © 2026 Fei Zheng-Ward

Identifiers: ISBN 979-8-89318-158-6 (eBook)
ISBN 979-8-89318-159-3 (paperback)
ISBN 979-8-89318-160-9 (hardcover)

Today is the day I go on an airplane.
I wonder what it will be like.

Sometimes new things can feel exciting

and a little different, too.

Before my trip, I help pack my bag.
Packing helps me feel ready.

What would you pack?

Point to or circle what you plan to bring with you.

Blanket   Stuffed animal   Book

Crayons   Snacks   Other:________________

We go to the airport, a big place that's busy and bright.

Once inside, we stand in line to get my boarding pass and check our bags.

How many bags do you have?

There are many friendly airport workers.

They are here to help kids like me.

Next comes the security check.

At the security check, airport workers look at
our things to help keep everyone safe.

I place my things in a bin.

The bin goes through a special machine that lets airport workers look inside the bags without opening them.

Cool, right?

What will they see inside *your* bag?

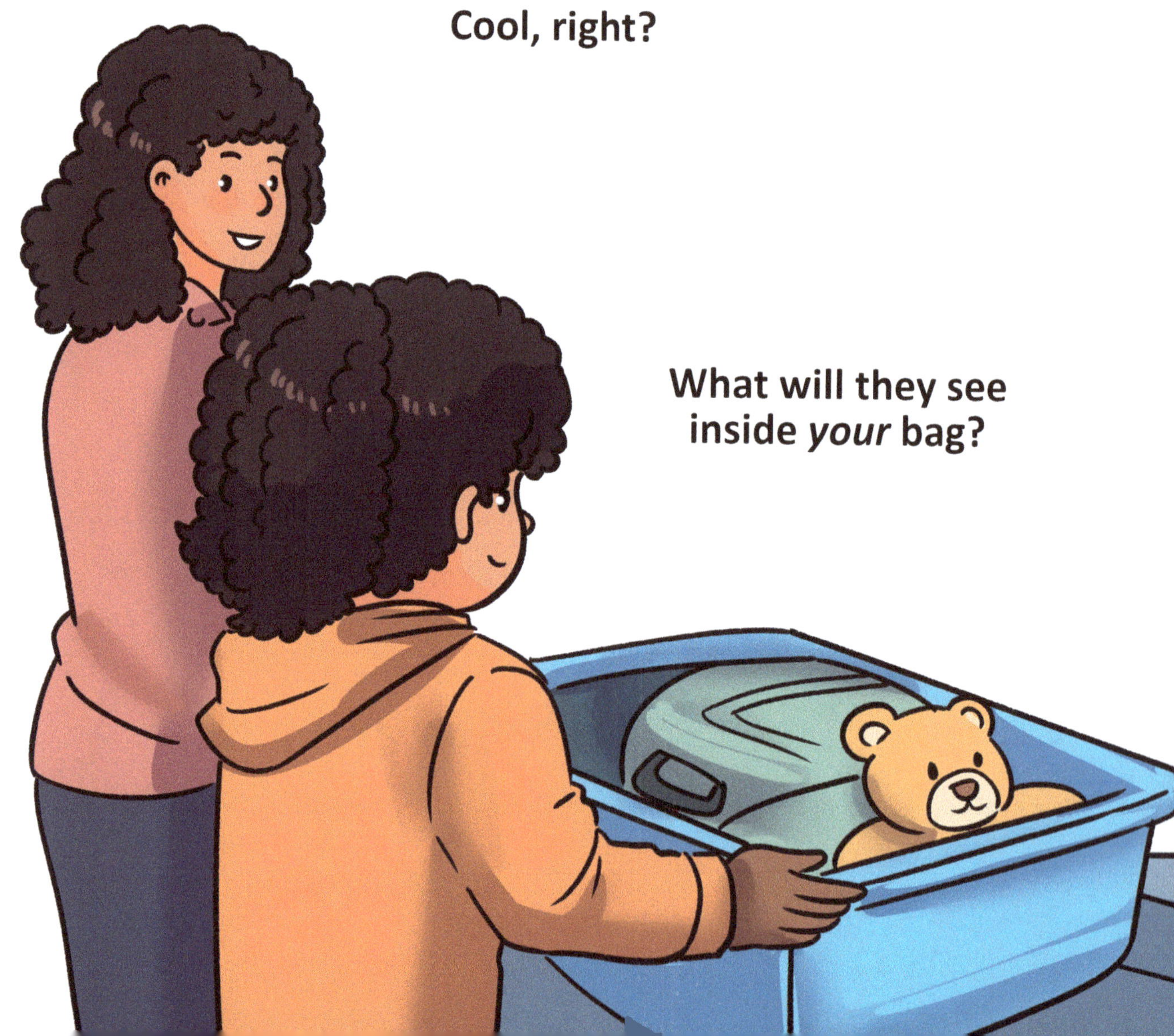

Then I walk through a special detector
to get closer to my plane.

Now we go to our gate,
and that is where I board the plane.

I look through big windows.

I can see airplanes outside!

What color is your airplane?

Soon, it's time for me to board.

I'm excited to see the inside of my plane.

Inside, there are friendly flight attendants.

They are kind, calm, and helpful.

Sometimes I can say hello to the pilot.

The pilot flies the airplane safely and brings us to new places.

Have you ever met a pilot?

YES __________

NO __________

I wonder if I will become a pilot one day.

I find my seat, and an adult can help me if I need it.
My bag goes under my seat or above my head.

Then I sit down and relax.
Just like in the car, I wear a seat belt to stay safe.

Can you spot these on the plane?

- ☐ windows
- ☐ a reading light
- ☐ a seat belt sign
- ☐ the bathroom sign

When the plane starts to move,
the flight attendants show safety rules.
They do this on every flight.

Everyone watches.

I am safe.

The plane goes faster and faster...

then lifts into the sky!

It may feel a little bumpy during takeoff.
That is normal.

Airplanes are
very safe.

I take a breath
in...
and blow it out
slowly.

Let's try it
together.

I am safe.

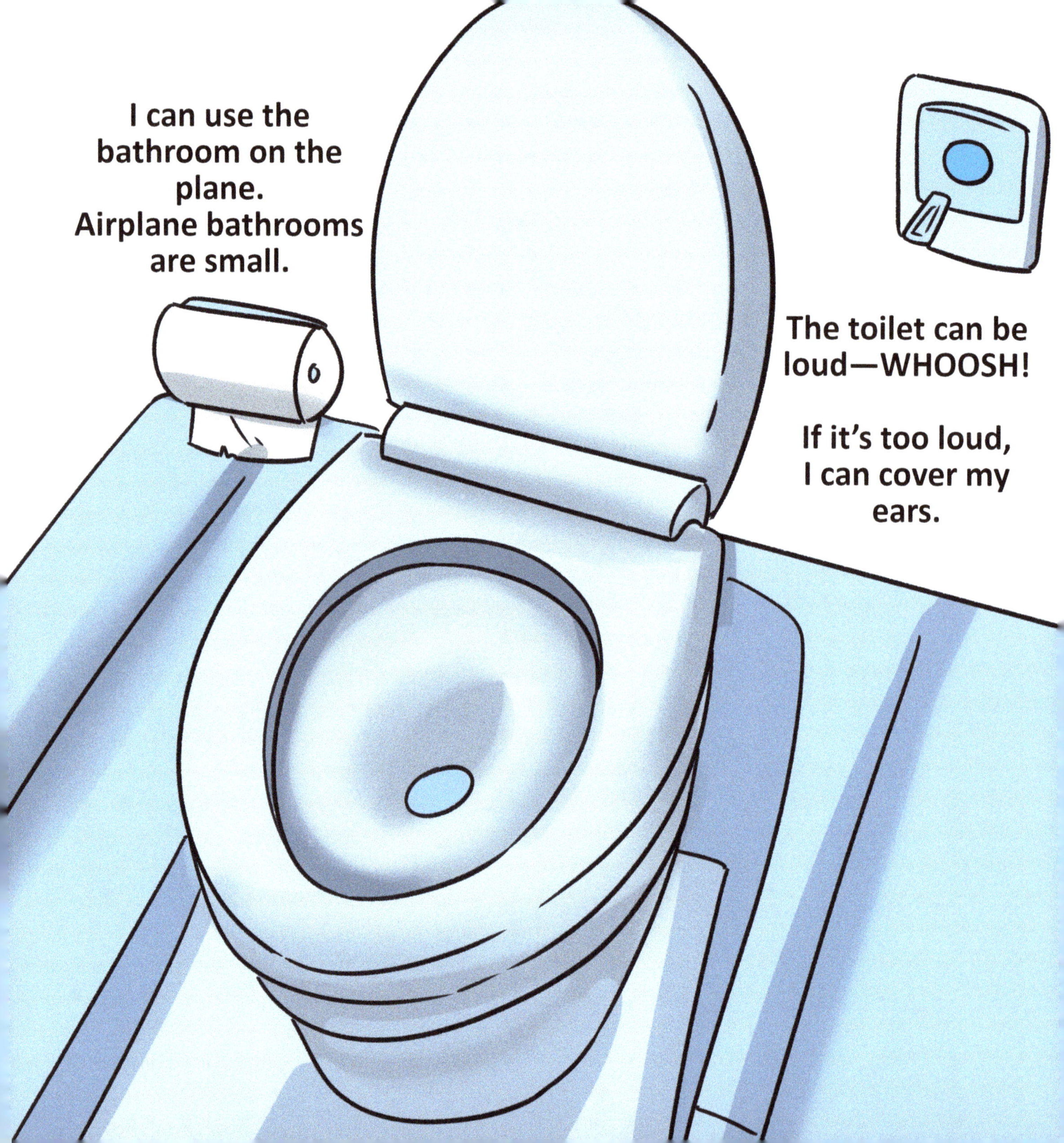
I can use the bathroom on the plane.
Airplane bathrooms are small.
The toilet can be loud—WHOOSH!
If it's too loud, I can cover my ears.

I wash my hands and
return to my seat.

During snack time, the flight attendants may bring
snacks and drinks.

What snacks and drinks do you hope to have?

CHIPS
PRETZELS

Sometimes my ears may feel funny.
That is normal and happens to many people.

I can yawn, chew, swallow, or suck on a lollipop to help my ears feel better. I can also gently blow my nose.

On the plane, I can read, watch a movie, color, or take a nap.

What would you like to do?

I can be kind to others by:

- staying in my seat when asked
- keeping my feet still
- using a quiet voice

When the plane lands, it may feel a little bumpy.
That is normal.

I wait my turn to get off.

I am safe.

We pick up our bags and head out.

Our adventure is just getting started!

I did it!

I flew on an airplane.

I'm proud of myself!

Where will your next adventure be?

Did your child enjoy this book?
If so, I would love to hear about it!

www.amazon.com/gp/product-review/B0FN76NRN1

For other book titles, please visit:

www.fzwbooks.com

Connect with the Author

email: books@fzwbooks.com
facebook/instagram: @FZWbooks

DINOSAUR
SEARCH AND FIND
By
Fei Zheng-Ward
Illustrated by
Nabila Amanda

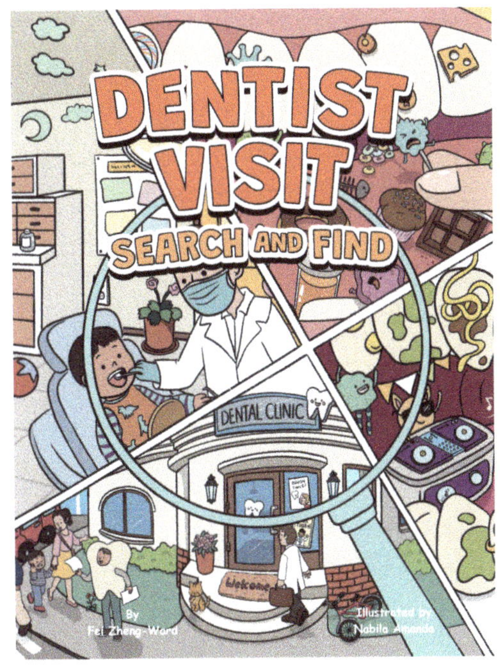

DENTIST VISIT
SEARCH AND FIND
DENTAL CLINIC
welcome
By
Fei Zheng-Ward
Illustrated by
Nabila Amanda

BEDTIME
SEARCH AND FIND
Goodnight Sleepy Animals
By
Fei Zheng-Ward
Illustrated by
Nabila Amanda

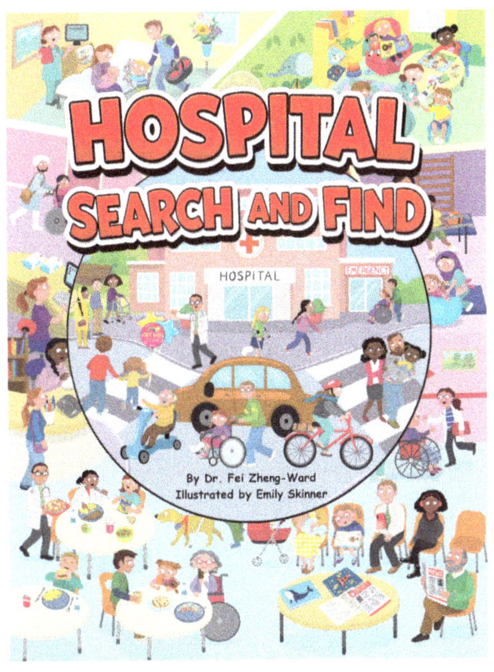

HOSPITAL
SEARCH AND FIND
HOSPITAL
EMERGENCY
By Dr. Fei Zheng-Ward
Illustrated by Emily Skinner